G·A·K · ·J·K

For
much-loved cats
and other small animals
laid in earth
nearby

PARS ET IN ILLIS

ROUND CHURCH STREE

Cutting across Cambridge

KINDERSLEY INSCRIPTIONS
IN THE CITY AND UNIVERSITY

Lida Lopes Cardozo Kindersley

AND

Thomas Sherwood

CARDOZO KINDERSLEY · CAMBRIDGE 2011

First published 2011
Reprinted 2013

Designed by Phil Treble, using the series layout designed by Eiichi Kono.

Photographs by Philip Moore and from the Cardozo Kindersley Archives.

Maps drawn by Fiona Boyd.

The book has been set in 12 pt Emilida, a typeface designed by Lida Lopes Cardozo Kindersley, digitised by ITA Kono Design, commissioned by Timothy Guy Design for EMI. The typeface was enhanced in 2010, with many OpenType features and attention to spacing, by Eben Sorkin.

Printed in the United Kingdom at the Lavenham Press Ltd.

ISBN-13: 978-1-107-64713-8 paperback

Copies available from:
Cambridge University Press Bookshop
1 Trinity Street
Cambridge CB2 1SZ
UK

Frontispiece: Kindersley street sign by the Round Church.

Contents

Introduction

Following on our 'Cutting through the Colleges', Cambridge University Press 2010, we go on a different journey: our work on inscriptions in stone and many other materials for the City, University and churches of Cambridge. And that is merely the story so far; the Workshop's orders always include local commissions among many others.

It is over 800 years ago that colleges began in Cambridge, and they are still very much places apart – independent foundations that treasure their individuality and autonomy. But soon they found they needed a common central body: the start of the University with a capital U.

Welsh slate from the Old Schools (see page 44)

HINC LUCEM ET POCULA SACRA

on this staircase, which forms part of the University's oldest building, the names are recorded of benefactors who have made possible the continuation of its ancient traditions of scholarship, learning and research

The first recorded chancellor, Hugh de Hottun, was elected by 1246. In time university departments grew up ('Schools' at first, for teaching and examining); together with an administration, now in the Old Schools. They all came to want lettering in order to inform, to commemorate, and to celebrate special occasions or places. Therefore much of the book is about this central (not college) university.

The City of Cambridge is naturally another entity, yet long intertwined with the university – and both very occasionally at war. Corpus Christi College was founded by the citizens, not by the usual aristocratic patron. And the city too has commissioned Kindersley work, from street signs to lettering for commerce. We reflect this interdependence in the lay-out of the book: the sections mix university and city pieces – together with church and churchyard memorials. There is a full list of churchyard/cemetery stones at the back.

'May fortune attend this house' – there is no scale design as Lida drew the inscription straight out onto the stone.

This is not a complete record of everything that has been done over 60 years – there is too much. It is a selective and practical guide, mainly to what can (or could) be seen in public. 'Could' has changed over the years: quite a number of pieces indoors, once accessible, are now behind security barriers. The text has to be your Ariel here.

We may think, innocently, that stone inscriptions are for ever. Churches and churchyards know this; but we have found that secular authorities are less mindful of their heritage pieces, and apt to do away with them. We have included archive illustrations in this book from among the more remarkable lost property.

Colleges and Addenbrooke's Hospital* are of course not here. And wait, why stop so rigidly at the city gates, are there not...? Yes, 'Cutting around Cambridgeshire' is to follow; it will also have the work outside the strict city boundary, such as in the Science Park. All these books express the concern that we must have a care for letters cut – and their wider values.

LLCK & TS

The main sections of the book divide Cambridge by its wards (in lieu of the former parishes): here and there the boundaries are crossed, to allow the most convenient groupings. So the start is centrally in Market ward; from there we move south-west to Trumpington, and then in an anti-clockwise spiral around the centre, finishing at Newnham in the west. Postcodes are occasionally given for easier location. The inside covers of the book show examples of private commissions.

The Workshop undertakes many private commissions, like this alphabet housed in Cambridge – Welsh slate, 2000.

* see 'Kindersley at Addenbrooke's Hospital' (Cardozo Kindersley 2000)

History of Cambridge street signs

(Extracted from David Kindersley: Optical letter spacing; Cambridge, 2001)

Shortly after the war, I think in 1947, Mr Crutchley, the University Printer, and I were horrified to wake up one morning to

find the unique and characterful cast-iron street names being removed from the centre of Cambridge. Furthermore they were being replaced by a particularly bad sample of Ministry of Transport lettering – equally badly spaced. It was believed that the new street signs were more legible and thus the change was justified. All praise goes to the City Engineer, who promptly put back the cast-iron signs when it was pointed out that at least it was doubtful whether the new signs were more legible than the old. Unfortunately the patterns from which the cast-iron

David Kindersley's M.o.T. alphabet is designed to be easily read, either white on black, or vice versa.

signs were cast had ceased to be available and new streets and
roads required name-plates. So it came about that I 'set-to-work'
designing a street name alphabet.

My first task was to visit the sign makers and to find out how
signs were made. By and large my design took into account the
limitations of casting
and particularly
stamping, but the
main feature was
the built-in system
of spacing. Here was
the greatest need.
It can be truly said
that sign makers
who were producing
direction signs, street name-plates and car numbers had, at that
time, no idea of spacing at all. This in part was due to a directive
from the Ministry of Transport who stated that no letter should
be closer than $\frac{1}{2}$ inch on car number plates.

My completed design for a street name alphabet was turned
down by the Cambridge Council and a fierce correspondence
arose in the local press. Ultimately my alphabet plus systems
of spacing for two other alphabets – 'Gill Sans' and 'Standard
M.o.T.' – were bought by the Ministry of Transport. Without
realizing it Cambridge chose my alphabet out of a catalogue and
after all my signs gradually appeared in the streets!

David Kindersley was judged 'a black-bearded lettercutter incapable of designing modern road or motorway signs'; even though this example shows that his capitals made for more elegantly legible road lettering than what we now have.

13

The start

It is January 1945, and David Kindersley is in the turmoil of moving to his new workshop in Barton, a village just outside Cambridge. For 6 months he has been in correspondence with a young widow whose husband, a Fellow of Trinity College, died quite suddenly aged only 28. She wants a 1 1/2 metre tall memorial cross of Cornish granite for his grave in Newmarket Road Cemetery; but the war is still on and things are not easy. A new letter in January: will he at least make and erect a wooden cross in oak as interim, just giving the initials R.A.L.S. with R.I.P. and dates ? And ready for her next visit to Cambridge in February ? Even in the midst of moving workshops, he does; and she writes how very much she liked it.

The inscribed granite memorial is a much larger problem in wartime. Masons from London write 'we really do not know when we should get the blocks or labour', from Cornwall 'owing to the loss of so many men, and the present number of orders on our books, we are unable...'. Another quarry in Cornwall is blunt: 'we do not supply the public with memorials... are you in the monumental trade?'.

It takes another year of negotiations until the cross is finished in April 1946. David Kindersley is 30 years old, and the venture of moving from High Wycombe in Buckinghamshire to Barton is perhaps beginning to look right. He had been Eric Gill's apprentice (1934–36) before setting out on his own (Sussex and Dorset); High Wycombe had been Gill's workshop, and his widow had asked David there in 1943. Once at Barton, David engaged two apprentices, and in his first year of 1945, there are 9 commissions, 2 within the village. By the end of 1946 there will be 27 new pieces; 1952 sees 43! But the 1946 Lendon Smith cross is his first and also large work for Cambridge: much admired by the family and college. The way ahead is set.

Growing up as Eric Gill's apprentice, David Kindersley learnt an architectural approach to everything he did, from drawing board to final work. Great stress was always laid on getting client and artisan to make a clear and comprehensive plan from the start.

Market (with Petersfield)

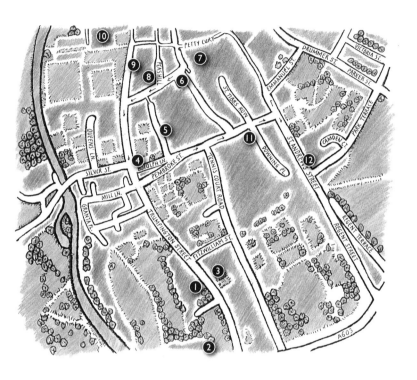

1. Fitzwilliam Museum
2. Engineering Department
3. Bridget's
4. St Botolph's Church
5. Free School Lane
6. Corn Exchange
7. Lion Yard
8. St Edward's Church
9. 11 King's Parade
10. Old Schools
11. Downing Street
12. St Andrew's Street

Fitzwilliam Museum

Starting from the new south entrance, you quickly reach the Armour gallery on the ground floor. Here three panels for MAJOR DONORS were cut directly into the existing wall of Larrys limestone in 2004.

When the museum began its new Courtyard scheme, the design of the benefactors' inscriptions, for newly devised wall spaces, was an integral part of the project. So these benefactors, high up on their limestone columns, do not have to compete with the ground-level armoury men for prime place: one enhances the other.

MAJOR DONORS TO
THE AMERICAN FRI
UNIVERSITY·ARTS A
RESEARCH BOARD·
DIANA BARING·MO
CAMBRIDGE CITY C
IN AMERICA·PAUL
JUDITH PORTRAIT·C
CHADWYCK·HEALE

DONALD AND MARY MELVILLE · TH[...]
MERCERS COMPANY · LISA MELTZ[...]
SARAH KINGSLEY-NEWMAN · JERG[...]
PEMBERTON · THE PEMBERTON F[...]
ANN ROBINSON · SIMON SAINSB[...]
NEVILLE SILVERSTON · KATE SMIT[...]
CHARLOTTE AND DENNIS STEVE[...]
TRINITY COLLEGE CAMBRIDGE · TH[...]
TRUSTHOUSE CHARITABLE FOUND[...]
JOAN UTTERIDGE · THE WOLFSO[...]
FOUNDATION

In the adjacent Near East gallery
a pair of engraved glass doors
is for THE GREAT BRITAIN
SASAKAWA FOUNDATION
FAN GALLERY (1987).
Further in are Cypriot Antiquities:
THIS GALLERY WAS
REFURBISHED...LEVENTIS...
is a Portland stone (1997), high on
the east wall. On again to the THE
EGYPTIAN COLLECTIONS
WERE CONSERVED – a 2006
Portland stone over a doorway in that gallery.

A pair of doors engraved in situ using a dentist's drill; on-the-spot work has the advantage of seeing at once how the design is to fit into the surroundings.

THIS GALLERY WAS REFURBISHED
THROUGH THE GENEROSITY OF
THE A G LEVENTIS FOUNDATION
AND WAS OPENED BY
HRH THE DUKE OF EDINBURGH KG KT
CHANCELLOR OF THE UNIVERSITY
MDCCCCXCVII

The subdued colours of these stones were chosen to reflect the hue of their galleries. For the Egyptian collection the use of a suitable red in the letters is a further echo.

THE EGYPTIAN COLLECTIONS
WERE CONSERVED AND RE-DISPLAYED
THROUGH THE GENEROSITY OF
THE HERITAGE LOTTERY FUND · THE GARFIELD
WESTON FOUNDATION · DCMS/WOLFSON
FOUNDATION FUND · THE GETTY FOUNDATION
THE TRUST HOUSE CHARITABLE FOUNDATION
AURELIUS CHARITABLE TRUST · RENAISSANCE
ISAAC NEWTON TRUST AND OTHER
CORPORATE & PRIVATE DONORS
MMVI

THESE GALLERIES HAVE BEEN CREATED
THROUGH THE GENEROSITY OF
The Museums and Galleries Improvement Fund
The Fitzwilliam Museum Trust
The Foundation for Sport and the Arts
The Earl Fitzwilliam Charitable Trust
The Henry Moore Foundation
The Merrin Gallery
The Chapman Charitable Trust
MDCCCCXCV

Although we prefer the upright position for cutting in the Workshop, when needs must we can work sitting, kneeling, on our haunches...

In the old entrance hall there are two early (1951) patterned glass windows with black capitals WAY OUT and arrow. Downstairs beneath this hall, left of the lavatories approach, THESE GALLERIES HAVE BEEN CREATED THROUGH THE GENEROSITY OF was cut in situ into the marble floor in 1996.

MVNIFICENTIA CAROLI BRINSLEY MARLAY, A.M. 1831-1912

BRINSLEY MARLAY

Upstairs at the south end of the Upper Marlay gallery, *MUNIFICENTIA CAROLI BRINSLEY MARLAY is a 1959 inscription in wood, high above a doorway; naming the portrait of a great 19th century benefactor. From there on to the Graham Robertson Room, where an inner office has a fine oval panel in Australian walnut (1955) – the benefactors celebrated here begin with WALFORD GRAHAM ROBERTSON.*

These rooms
built and furnished
from the benefactions of
WALFORD GRAHAM ROBERTSON
OSCAR CHARLES RAPHAEL
EDWARD EVELYN BARRON
ROWLAND HARRY BIFFEN
were completed in
1955

For this walnut panel to have a gilded inscription, the letters have to be sealed first, and then varnished with goldsize before gold leaf is applied.

There used to be a coin collection with an aptly circular glass inscription THE CRIPPS GALLERY 1985 – we show the design here.

At the end of this lettering tour two quite unassuming pieces demand special attention. Of the many WAY OUT (and other direction) signs made for the museum in the 1950s, a charming small 1951 one remains: en route from the European to the Japanese Pottery galleries. It is gold paint on blue leatherette with hardwood backing;

The blue leatherette is stretched over hardwood, and the letters carried out in gold.

David Kindersley complained at the time about finding leatherette 'quite unobtainable'. In the grounds outside, to the right of the path to the new entrance, a 2008 Portland stone is in the lawn – ANTHONY TOOTAL 1947–2005. It commemorates a man who was instrumental in the museum's developments across the millennium (particularly the new 2004 Courtyard) and much loved.

A light-coloured stone like Portland is good for a flat out-of-doors location: the years add grit in the letters, and thus legibility.

David Kindersley is drawing lettering freehand on the metal, before drilling out each of the individual dots that will make up a whole letter.

Department of Engineering & Bridget's

Just south of the museum along Trumpington Street: a driveway leads to the reception building. The open courtyard inside it has a large metal fountain DESIGNED AND CARRIED OUT BY PETER LYON; all the sides of the triangular base are inscribed in capitals (1981). The fountain is TO THE MEMORY OF FIONA, LADY BAKER, WHOSE CARE & CONCERN FOR ALL WHO WORKED HERE & FOR THEIR FAMILIES MEANT SO MUCH TO THE DEPARTMENT OF ENGINEERING FROM 1945 TO 1968. These capitals are

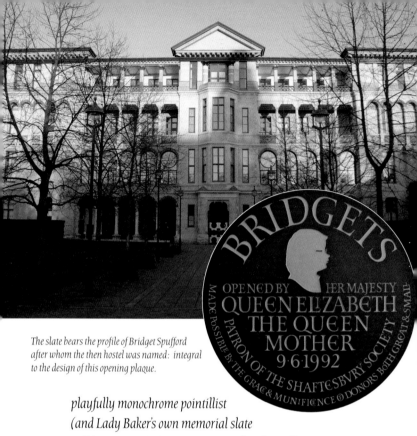

The slate bears the profile of Bridget Spufford after whom the then hostel was named: integral to the design of this opening plaque.

playfully monochrome pointillist (and Lady Baker's own memorial slate will be seen again in Trumpington churchyard).

Bridget's Hostel for disabled students is no longer, but its 1992 Welsh slate for the opening by the Queen Mother can still be seen at 24A Trumpington Street, opposite the Fitzwilliam, inside the University's Disability Resource Centre. The hostel had a touching 1992 Welsh slate CHARLIE'S GARDEN for the favourite haunt of a disabled student – he died a year after graduation, and the stone and its 1994 replacement have also gone.

The Workshop was asked (1987) to add 'and of his loving wife
KATHARINE DARWIN' to an existing memorial for Charles
Galton Darwin (physicist grandson of Charles Darwin and
Master of Christ's College); on the inside North wall near the exit
to the rear churchyard. Ask to be let out here for a quiet discovery
of a lovely place, and make for the south wall bordering St
Botolph's Lane. Hidden under shrubs, there is a rectangular
Welsh blue-black slate (1985) for ARTHUR LLEWELLYN
ARMITAGE, President of Queens' College and Vice-Chancellor.
His widow commissioning the stone wondered about having
her name on it also, but decided on a blank space at the time.
15 years later the stone was cleaned by the Workshop, and then
completed in 2006: 'and his wife JOAN KENYON'.

The letters are
painted off-white,
so they have the
freshly-cut quality
as when first cut.

27

*Obliquely opposite the back of St Botolph's, pause in Free School
Lane to wonder at 'Here in 1897 at the old Cavendish Laboratory
J. J. THOMSON discovered the electron...' – an oval 1997
Welsh slate.*

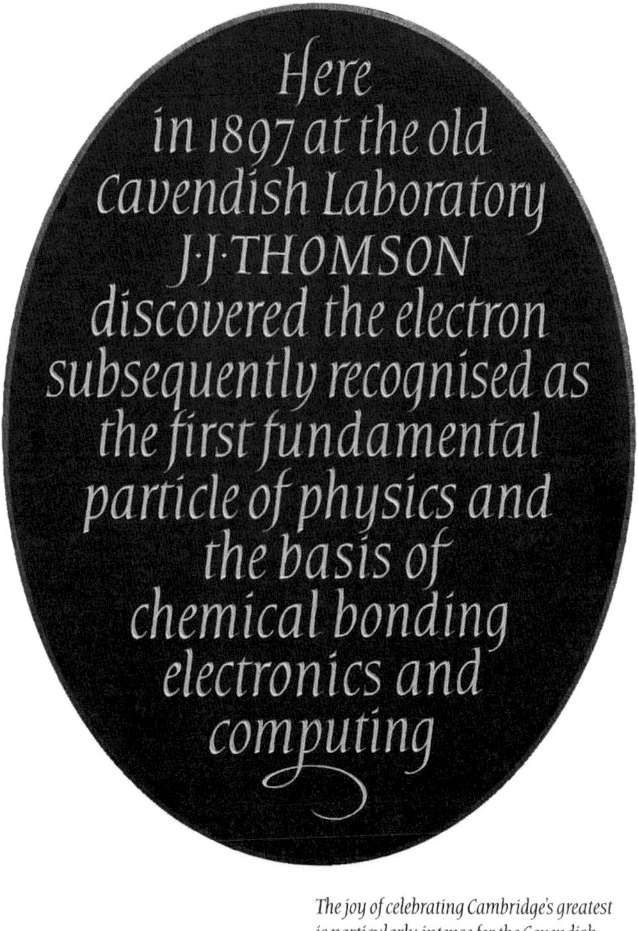

Here
in 1897 at the old
Cavendish Laboratory
J·J·THOMSON
discovered the electron
subsequently recognised as
the first fundamental
particle of physics and
the basis of
chemical bonding
electronics and
computing

*The joy of celebrating Cambridge's greatest
is particularly intense for the Cavendish
Laboratory – and for us.*

SPONSORED BY
CAMLAB
IN THE NAME OF
ROBERT HIRSCH

Corn Exchange
Not readily accessible except to audiences, the right-hand box
furthest from the stage has a 1995 green slate on the back wall ...
IN THE NAME OF ROBERT HIRSCH.

Lion Yard

Commercial development of this area has courted controversy for decades, since the 1970s demise of old Petty Cury has been followed by new bulldozing this century. We have our own chisels out on this score, with much work from 1950–80 all gone now. Interesting things are lost here. Among them is the 1980 opening of the Magistrates' Courthouse, a beechwood plaque. And worse: a remarkable 230 cm high cylindrical column of glass-reinforced concrete and granite from 1976. This bore the names of Aldermen, Councillors and Chief Officers principally concerned with the redevelopment of Lion Yard from 1968 to 1975.

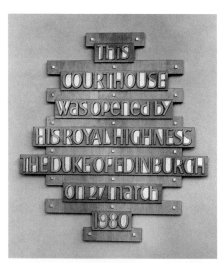

Every wooden letter was cut out by hand and put onto strips; the fixing points for these strips are among the decorative studs. Gold leaf was applied to some of the counters (the inside spaces of letters). This is boldly unconventional lettering – the County architect Peter Arthur was an ever encouraging influence on these experiments.

This column is not just a list of people: it is a playful solution toward making an entertaining roll-call. Letters were cut out and stuck on a former before being cast in glass-reinforced concrete and granite. This was to guard against vandalism; and indeed the column was never attacked – until the day it was quietly removed.

But fine pieces remain. The 1975 opening of Lion Yard by Princess Anne is marked by an oval Welsh slate high on a wall facing east, nearly opposite the entrance to the church of St Andrew the Great. In Petty Cury itself, head for the Boots' entrance and look up right. A 1978 clock hangs out: its face and the elegant brickwork backing it a David Kindersley design. It was originally for the H. Samuel firm; changing owners over the years have left bad marks.

LION YARD
OPENED BY
HER ROYAL HIGHNESS
THE PRINCESS ANNE
4TH DECEMBER 1975
Developed jointly by
The City of Cambridge
&
Ravenseft Properties Limited

This is a riven slate with the arms of Cambridge raised on top, fully painted and gilded, as is the shield at the bottom.

Quite different solutions were needed for the formal 1975 opening and the 2010 repeat by Princess Anne: note the elongated sans serif lettering of the glass panel for the 21st century – a 35 year bridge for the new library's modern setting.

The Library was opened by Her Royal Highness The Princess Anne 4th December 1975

The City Library inside the Grand Arcade was first opened, again by Princess Anne in 1975; the oval blue-black slate celebrating this has been rehung. This is because she came to re-open the remodelled library in 2010: a glass panel with strikingly elongated lettering was designed for the occasion. Both pieces are reached via the entrance on the first floor; you turn left and head straight for them, on walls by reading bays near windows. At the north end of this floor, in the children's section, a pillar carries a rectangular brass plate for PAT GRAY 'a teacher' (2000).

In memory of
PAT GRAY
1919 - 1997
a teacher

We painted the letters white, so they will show better as the brass tarnishes to a darker colour over the years.

The material used for the clock face is Travertine marble. It no longer has the Kindersley lettering for H. Samuel over it. This dandelion clock design (note the gilded hour lines with their triangles) is mirrored in the carving of the brickwork behind.

33

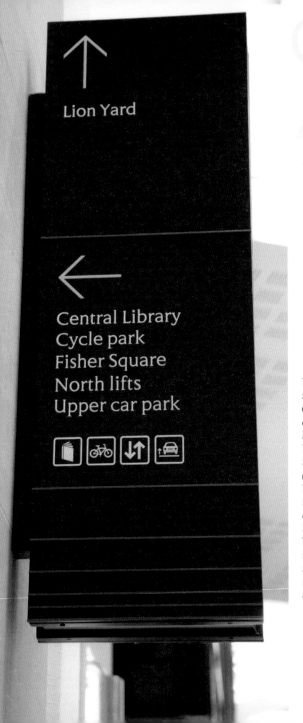

The Grand Arcade team specifically wanted a Cambridge alphabet based on David Kindersley's M.o.T. street lettering. This was ideal because of its elegance and legibility (the story is on page 12). This face, designed for metal road signs, needed a lower case and an italic letter form added; called 'Grand Arcade' it has been used throughout this large shopping mall. Now it is freely available, as a digitized typeface.

All the lettering for the new Grand Arcade was designed by the Workshop; and its 2008 opening is recorded on a rectangular glass panel, just to the left of the arcade's John Lewis entrance.

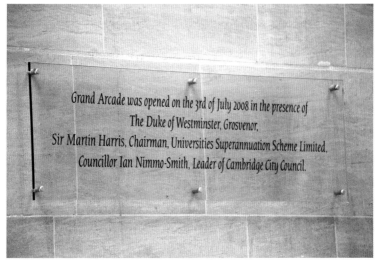

Grand Arcade was opened on the 3rd of July 2008 in the presence of
The Duke of Westminster, Grosvenor,
Sir Martin Harris, Chairman, Universities Superannuation Scheme Limited,
Councillor Ian Nimmo-Smith, Leader of Cambridge City Council.

Because this is not signage the letters here are different from the rest of the arcade. For this special occasion we chose a less formal and more free-flowing face, also designed in the Workshop and named Emilida. The red inscription was silk-screened in reverse on the back of the glass.

The initial letters of the Grand Arcade illustrate David Kindersley's 'optical centres'.
The vertical bars of the gates are placed to accord with this optical letter spacing system.
For more read his 'Optical letter spacing' (Cambridge, Cardozo Kindersley 2001).

ST EDWARD
KING & MARTYR

This Parish Church
has stood here for
over 800 years
& was the cradle of the
English Reformation

Today it combines
respect for tradition
with relevance to
modern life

The Book of
Common Prayer is used here

St Edward's church

*After the church gate but before entering by the door, bear right
and then left down a short path, to a flat green slate in the
ground for SIR GEOFFREY INGRAM TAYLOR and his wife
(1993). You have already met him as one of the Trinity College
greats, with a brass plate of his own in that antechapel – but
only if you read 'Cutting through the Colleges'!*

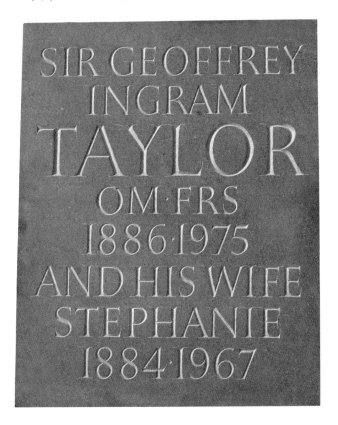

Within the church two stones give an insight into Reformation horror and triumph. An oval Portland stone (1955) on the inside north wall is 'to honour those from this parish who in the years 1523–25 met near by at the White Horse Inn and there sought out the principles of the English Reformation...THOMAS BILNEY... ROBERT BARNES... HUGH LATIMER'. They argued the need for an English bible, and all became martyrs. Hugh Latimer was University Chaplain at the time, then Bishop of Worcester (1535) and a prisoner in the Tower (1539 & 1546); restored briefly to favour as court preacher, he was burned at the stake outside Balliol College, Oxford (1555).

The panel for the lettering is sunk into the stone, leaving a raised moulding; this means hard preparatory work in chiselling down the surface, followed by fine rubbing. Only then can the letters be drawn out, cut and painted.

To the Glory of God
and to honour those from this Parish
who in the years 1523 to 1525
met near by at the White Horse Inn
and there sought out
the principles of the English Reformation

THOMAS BILNEY + 1531
ROBERT BARNES + 1540
HUGH LATIMER + 1555

who through faith quenched
the violence of fire.

The Portland stone frames the Cornish slate inscription, and the moulding eases it into its surroundings. A stone's setting is a major influence on what we choose to design.

Triumph: a Cornish Delabole slate with Portland stone moulding (1947), to be found on a south-facing pillar in the south aisle. It is for EDWARD LIVELY and RICHARD THOMPSON, translators for the King James Bible (1604–11). There were 'companies' in Westminster, Oxford and Cambridge involving 56 scholar-translators, to produce 'the only great work of art ever created by committee'.

There is also an oval Nabresina marble (1964) on the inside north wall, 'in loving memory of' a Trinity Hall Master & wife, HENRY ROY DEAN and IRENE.

Following the Bilney/Barnes/Latimer precedent in Portland, the names are picked out in red on this marble.

11 King's Parade

Leaving the church, in King's Parade, look up and to the left of no. 11. CHARLES LAMB LODGED HERE AUGUST 1819 said a small rectangular stone tablet that was disintegrating 40 years ago. David Kindersley cut a new slate in 1971.

The original red sandstone inscription.

Old Schools

The University's administrative headquarters, behind the Senate House, have a splendid staircase leading up to the Vice-Chancellor's office (not public). A large oval Welsh slate (1997) at its base explains the purpose of an ever growing gallery of rectangular slates lining the walls on the way up. They record benefactors of the

Detail from the oval on page 7.

University, updated and added to in the years since. On the first floor landing two 1997 Welsh slates are for the Cambridge Foundation: its chairmen and benefactors.

BENEFACTORS

The Cultural and Arts Management Trust · The Hauser-Raspe Foundation · The Hong Kong Cambridge Medical School Liaison charity · Hamid Dhiya Jafar · The Government of India · Dr William M W Mong · Randall Dillard · James Hudleston · Dr Alan Reece · Mark Pigott · Walters Kundert charitable Trust · The Kirby Laing Foundation · Richard Enschmann · Professor Philip Gnerson · Guy Whittaker · Dr Leonard Polonsky

BENEFACTORS

Dame Stephanie Shirley · The Winton charitable Foundation · His Majesty Sultan Qaboos bin Said Sultan of Oman · James & Jane Wilson · Brian Buckley · The Gillespie Family Trust · Leslie W K Chung · Dr Ramon Jenkins · Kyoko Gledhill, in memory of David Gledhill · Cancer Research UK · John Osborn · Professor Y W Loke · Winston Churchill Foundation of the United States · Walter & Rosemary Scott

BENEFACTORS

Dr Denys Armstrong · Steven Edwards · Dr Donald Kellaway · Graham Kushion · the Kavli Foundation · Gaylord and Dorothy Donnelley Foundation · Sir Evelyn de Rothschild · The Coexist Foundation · The de Botton family in memory of Gilbert de Botton · The Cadbury family · Countess de Brye · Alwaleed Bin Jalal Foundation · The A G Leventis Foundation · Professor Carl Djerassi · The MAVA Fondation

The Cambridge Foundation with its chairmen and benefactors is a continuing series of slates that have given this fine staircase new purpose.

In the ground floor entrance hall
there is a similarly expanding series
of glass plates for the Guild of Cambridge Benefactors. They
began in 2009, and a glass plate above a doorway shows the
arms and motto of the University, used by the Guild.

46

The Smuts Memorial Desk for the Senate House, given by Christ's College, had the Latin explanation cut into the wood by David Kindersley in 1953.

The inset shows an extract from the dyeline print; exceptionally made in full size for the long inscription in wood, demanding a rigid classic design. Normally only a small-scale design is made, because when it comes to actually doing the work, we need the freedom to fine-tune our ideal for the inscription. That allows us to make changes at every stage of drawing out, cutting and finishing.

At its eastern end, opposite the hotel, is the arched entrance to a University site. Make straight for a rectangular yellowish Ancaster stone on the big wall ahead, DEPARTMENT OF PLANT SCIENCES, recording the centenary of the building (2004). It features a double helix – Cambridge!

Letters were not painted here: the weathering of the Ancaster stone means they become more legible over time.

In this department itself, for a third floor laboratory, there is a red-lettered glass plaque recording the 2009 opening; which was done by the Vice-Chancellor because the Duke of Edinburgh was indisposed. So a new version had to be designed and made in a hurry.

On the same site, east of the entrance approach, is the McDonald Institute for Archaeological Research. On its outside left at ground level is the foundation stone in blue-black Cumbrian slate (1992). It bears a triskelion – the three-legged

Isle of Man/McDonald symbol. There is also a large Ketton stone naming the institute above the entrance, carved in situ (1994). The 1994 opening by the Prince of Wales is commemmorated by a rectangular Welsh slate in the entrance hall.

FOUNDER
D·M·McDONALD
BSc · MB · ChB

THIS STONE WAS LAID BY
MRS W·M· McDONALD
4TH JUNE 1992

It is not just the triskelion which is special here: each stone carries details designed for a specific commisssion. So note the ligatures of *DO* in the names, of *TH* and *UN* in the date, of *NE* and *WA* in the fourth line; in the same line there is 'nesting' of *TH*, *TO* and *LAI*.

There is more ligature and nesting work here – the inside and outside stones are at one. The *AE* diphthong is something different, bound together since ancient times. Both these slates have their letters painted off-white.

THE McDONALD INSTITUTE
FOR ARCHÆOLOGICAL RESEARCH
WAS OPENED BY H·R·H
THE PRINCE OF WALES
ON THE 25TH NOVEMBER 1994

McDONALD INSTITUTE
FOR ARCHÆOLOGICAL RESEARCH

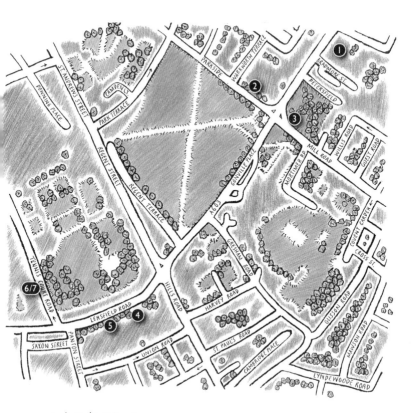

1. Anglia Ruskin University
2. Police Station
3. Mill Road
4. Scott Polar Research Institute
5. Chemistry Laboratories
6. Biochemistry Department
7. Wellcome Trust

More of the couplings already seen on the slates'
letters, but cut in situ here, to make the inscription
part of the building's architecture.

51

No. 50 is opposite the old Police Station, and called JANUS HOUSE – a colourful 1968 panel has the name cut into Ashburton marble, with two-faced Janus as a bronze relief medallion inset.

The letters were cut in situ into marble and gilded with gold leaf. David modelled Janus' head in clay; it was cast in bronze and then fixed into a chiselled down circular recess.

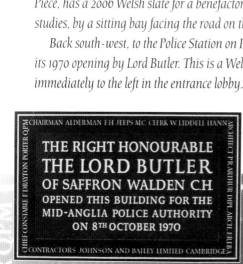

> LEE SKINNER-YOUNG
> 1924-2001
> Benefactor of Shakespeare Studies
> at Anglia Ruskin University

This slate has the name picked out in gold, and letters below painted white.
The name is in italic capitals, which allows for vigorous flourishing.

East Road

Anglia Ruskin University's building, a little north-east of Parker's Piece, has a 2006 Welsh slate for a benefactor of Shakespeare studies, by a sitting bay facing the road on the first floor.

Back south-west, to the Police Station on Parker's Piece, and its 1970 opening by Lord Butler. This is a Welsh blue-black slate immediately to the left in the entrance lobby.

The frieze of this slate has the benefactors in v-cut letters, whereas those of the central panel are raised.

> CHAIRMAN ALDERMAN F.H. JEEPS M.C. CLERK W. LIDDELL HANN
> CHIEF CONSTABLE F. DRAYTON PORTER Q.P.M.
> ARCHITECT P.R. ARTHUR DIP. ARCH. F.R.I.B.A
> THE RIGHT HONOURABLE
> THE LORD BUTLER
> OF SAFFRON WALDEN C.H.
> OPENED THIS BUILDING FOR THE
> MID-ANGLIA POLICE AUTHORITY
> ON 8TH OCTOBER 1970
> CONTRACTORS JOHNSON AND BAILEY LIMITED CAMBRIDGE

And back yet again to the big traffic junction and Mill Road, where there is a wooden shelter on the edge of the green. It has a 1951 teakwood inscription above, ALEX WOOD MEMORIAL. This was commissioned by the Cambs. and Hunts. Welfare of Youth and Band of Hope Union. Its letterhead explains the aims: '...the teaching of temperance and self-control as essential to a full Christian life, and the education of children and young people with respect to alcohol, gambling, impurity and other social evils'. Ah tempora!

The overhang of the roof has given the wooden panel protection from the weather; so it has lasted well over some 60 years.

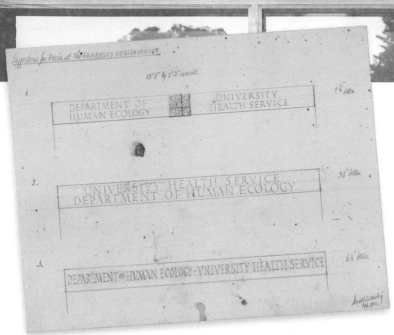

Further south at Fenners, there was once the Department of Human Ecology and the University Health Service. They had 1952 teak inscriptions, all gone.

The use of italic letters for 'of' cheers up this long line. David Kindersley offered a choice of designs – which he rarely did and we still hardly ever do.

UNIVERSITY HEALTH SERVICE

The Local Examinations Syndicate in Hills Road has a 1985 Cumbrian green slate for the opening of the Frank Wild Building, no longer visitable.

The
FRANK WILD
BUILDING
Opened 29 May 1985 by
SIR JOHN BURGH
K·C·M·G C·B
*Director-General of the
British Council*

Lensfield Road

The Scott Polar Research Institute houses the world's largest polar library. Upstairs a 1998 Ketton stone lintel, in three slabs, names the SHACKLETON MEMORIAL LIBRARY. The entrance to this part of the library is by a pair of glass doors, engraved with lettering and profiles for Ernest and Edward Shackleton (Ernest the father's exploits in the Antarctic being the more famous).

The outside frieze naming the building gave us the inspiration for these three heavy Ketton stones over the doors. They were carved and gilded in the Workshop, then fixed firmly in position over the engraved glass doors.

*   Also from 1998 and in similar style, a single glass door to the Polar Archive commemorates Thomas Manning (Arctic explorer, scientist and author).*

This name is less
well known than the
Shackletons of the
paired glass doors,
but Manning was
a remarkably versatile
and distinguished
man.

This building
was opened by
Her Royal Highness
Princess Margaret
on the sixth day
of November 1958

The University's Chemistry Laboratories, just west, have the building's opening by Princess Margaret on a Trani marble immediately to the left of the entrance steps. The stone dates from 1959, actually a year after the event. On the way back to the road, look for a sculpture on the wall facing the road, near the corner. A 1958 Ancaster stone beneath has the name of the laboratories in bold capitals, to match the stark relief above.

It is important for lettering to be in tune with its subject.

Flourishes spell celebration but need care – see the page 113 caption for comments.

THIS
BUILDING
WAS OPENED *on*
22 NOVEMBER
1997 *by*
DR FREDERICK
SANGER
OM·FRS

The Department of Biochemistry
records its grateful thanks to
the benefactors who have made
this building possible
THE WELLCOME TRUST
THE WOLFSON FOUNDATION
PETER & PAULA BECKWITH
TE KIRBY LAING FOUNDATION
ST JOHN'S COLLEGE
TRINITY COLLEGE
AMERICAN FRIENDS OF
CAMBRIDGE UNIVERSITY
UNIVERSITY OF CAMBRIDGE
AND MANY ALUMNI

The two slate panels
are set in a recess of
the wall; in the upper
note the WA ligature
and italicized 'on',
achieving correct
proportions for this
line.

Not far from Lensfield Road, up some steps to the west, the Biochemistry Department has a new building. A 1998 Welsh slate in the entrance hall records its opening by Nobel's FREDERICK SANGER; a second slate has the benefactors.

Opposite is the Wellcome Trust Centre for for Stem Cell Research and another entrance lobby with opening and benefactors' commemoration. These are 2006 glass plaques with blue lettering.

Bridget's Hostel for disabled students which used to be in this road has its opening stone preserved in Trumpington Street (see under Department of Engineering on page 26).

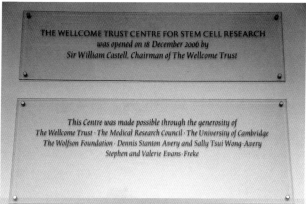

THE WELLCOME TRUST CENTRE FOR STEM CELL RESEARCH
was opened on 18 December 2006 by
Sir William Castell, Chairman of The Wellcome Trust

This Centre was made possible through the generosity of
The Wellcome Trust · The Medical Research Council · The University of Cambridge
The Wolfson Foundation · Dennis Stanton Avery and Sally Tsui Wong-Avery
Stephen and Valerie Evans-Freke

Trumpington

Botanic Garden
'Not up in place for view' is the refrain here too, alas, but this may change in time. There is a grand Clipsham stone carving of the University of Cambridge arms (1957); and from 1971 an elongated Westmorland green slate celebrating the benefactions of *REGINALD RADCLIFFE CORY*. The Latin tag here about 'if you seek a monument, look around you' is of course famously for Christopher Wren at St Paul's.

These arms are illustrated in Heather Child's 'Heraldic Design' (London, G. Bell 1965) as an exemplar of heraldic carving. So no comment on current neglect; we show the original state from an archive picture.

To commemorate with gratitude the benefactions of
REGINALD RADCLIFFE CORY 1871-1934
SI MONVMENTVM REQVIRIS CIRCVMSPICE

This slate had to be propped up on a chair because the building bearing it has gone – oh Sir Christopher!

65

Everyday traffic and direction signs can be uplifting.

Chaucer Road

The MRC Cognition and Brain Sciences Unit at no.15 has pillars facing the road with IN & OUT directions, and MRC (2005). Inside on the first floor is a 2001 glass plaque for the opening of the West Wing.

THE WEST WING OF THE MRC COGNITION & BRAIN SCIENCES UNIT
OPENED BY THE CHIEF EXECUTIVE OF THE MRC
PROFESSOR SIR GEORGE RADDA CBE FRS ON 24 SEPTEMBER 2001

The face used for the glass panel is Gill Sans – another reminder of the Workshop's long master-apprentice tradition.

Cambridge University Press (Shaftesbury Road)
The University Printer Brooke Crutchley and David Kindersley
met in the early 1940s; the Workshop's move to Barton in 1945
began a long-lasting tie with the Press.

*David Kindersley standing by
large blue letters which were cut
out of marine plywood and then
treated with 8 coats of paint.
They were fixed individually and
carefully spaced. The central
cross of the coat of arms is one
piece of wood, about 2 metres tall;
the four quarters with lions gilded
were fixed separately.*

The alphabet Meliorissimo is versatile: it can be used at almost any size in any material.

INTAKE ROOM
DANGER
HIGH VOLTAGE

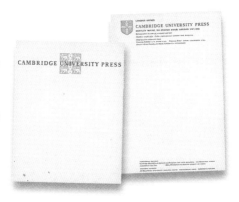

David Kindersley made a new design based on Hermann Zapf's typeface Melior, and called it Meliorissimo. It was used on, and in, throughout the Press buildings.

This was particularly active between 1961 and 1981; a special alphabet 'Meliorissimo' was designed for all Press buildings, stationery, signs, vans etc. (1964). It showed CAMBRIDGE UNIVERSITY PRESS in the appropriate Cambridge hue, and with a coat of arms; only one warehouse (on the southern fringe of the site) now retains these large blue capitals. Elsewhere there is the new corporate branding. In the old headquarters at the Pitt Building in Trumpington Street, the Workshop carved the Press name into the reception desk.

Letters cut straight into the wood: an assortment of razor sharp woodcarver's chisels are needed for this, quite different from a stonecutter's kit.

1939 1945

K·F·BAINES   Cambs. Regt.
H·F·H·GIGNEY Royal Air Force
W·J·HOBSON   Royal Artillery
R·E·MILLER   Essex Regt.
F·D·C·NEGUS   Home Guard
B·B·NEWELL   Royal Air Force
H·ODELL   Royal Air Force
F·L·PRATT   Royal Armd Corps
K·R·SEWELL   Royal Air Force
W·R·STARNS   Royal Air Force

Their name liveth for evermore

In 1948 a walnut panel was commissioned as a War Memorial for WWII staff. Brooke Crutchley first writes to David Kindersley: 'I think the Syndics may jib at a three-figure sum' – so it cost £85 and can be seen in a Printing House foyer.

This classic design is simpler than the 1950 walnut war memorial in Shire Hall (see page 107) – and no less affecting.

In the entrance hall of this building there are rectangular Welsh
slates for openings by the Vice-Chancellor J. S. BOYS SMITH
(1963) and 'The extension of THE UNIVERSITY PRINTING
HOUSE... DAVID WILLIAMS...' (1996).

An interesting addition to all this work for the Press is
a series of book jackets from the 1950s/60s. The designs for
GREEK INSCRIPTIONS (1958), DESIGN IN BRITISH
INDUSTRY (1956), and a 1956 Welsh slate ON THE
POETRY OF KEATS are illustrated. Further designs
were done for the New York division (1967) to adorn their
publicity material.

The 33 years
separating these two
slates make for
interesting differences
in the approach to
italic lettering across
this span.

This building was opened by
the Vice-Chancellor of the University
THE REVEREND J.S.BOYS SMITH
Master of Saint John's College
24 October 1963

The extension of
THE UNIVERSITY PRINTING HOUSE
was opened by
The Vice-chancellor of the University of Cambridge
PROFESSOR SIR DAVID WILLIAMS QC·DL
on Friday 27 September 1996

Every 20 years or so there is a clamour for 'doing up' Eric Gill's monument; our persuasion is to leave well alone, though David Kindersley added WWII names of course.

Trumpington village

The Portland stone War Memorial on the High Street opposite Bidwells is by Eric Gill; in 1947 David Kindersley cut 8 additional names from the Second World War into the south face.

Bidwells commissioned lettering from the Workshop between 1969–82, still seen all over the building and car park.

IN MEMORY
OF
REGINALD
GEORGE
SMITH
1912 – 1972

Rest in the Lord

Trumpington church

The south-west corner of the first churchyard is rich Workshop
territory: nine slates are on the walls, and one headstone against
the west wall in the corner (*REGINALD GEORGE SMITH,*
Portland stone, 1973). The 1980 green slate for *FIONA THE
LADY BAKER & LORD BAKER* connects with the fountain
inscription at the Department of Engineering (under Market
ward on page 25). All the names are in the list at the end.

*This is a green slate;
others in this plot are
blue/grey. All have
this stone's impervious
quality in common, and
last extremely well.*

*Portland stone weathers and ages
attractively – this stone is even more
charming three decades on.
However... (see page 76)*

Trumpington cemetery

This is at the corner of Shelford and Hauxton roads. Members of the PEMBERTON family have a 1962 Portland stone memorial near the end of the central path on the right, added to in 1972. And obliquely opposite across this path, to the south, is a large 170 cm tall ledger stone on the ground, a Welsh slate on a Portland stone plinth. Originally there was an old York stone here for Sir GEORGE DARWIN, Plumian Professor of Astronomy (he was the great Charles' second son), and his wife MAUD DU PUY. In 1950 GWEN RAVERAT asked David Kindersley to make a new inscription for her parents' memorial, in a letter with a charming sketch. After her death the replacement slate was commissioned for the three of them (1958).

The comments on delightful Portland weathering, made for GEORGE SMITH (on the previous page), apply equally here, but over time there are costs in legibility.

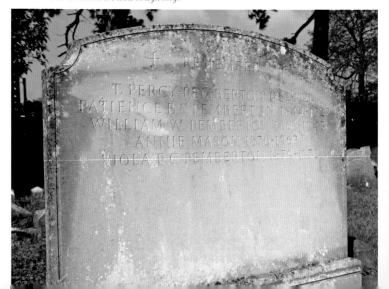

Tel. 56178
The Old Granary,
Silver Street,
Cambridge.

Dear Mr Kindersley

Do you cut inscriptions on tombstones ever? We wanted to see what having the names etc cut on a stone in Trumpington Cemetery – it is my parents' grave. The stone has been there a long time, but my father's name was only painted on one side; my mother's name is to be added now. We thought to make a clean start & have both their names cut on the clean side, & have the paint scraped off the other side. If this is anyway possible, could you ring me up, or perhaps come & see me about it & settle what is to be done. There is no great hurry about it, of course. I hope you can do it, as I want good plain lettering –

Yours sincerely
Gwen Raverat

Understanding what is in the client's mind is essential for any commission. Gwen Raverat, herself a gifted artist and writer, grasped this at once: her letter is a lovely example of how well it can be put.

Coleridge & Queen Edith

Michael Young Centre (Purbeck Road)
Glass nameplates for six buildings were done on this National Extension College site: NEVILL MOTT, GEOFFREY HUBBARD, BRIAN JACKSON, SPECTRUM, IMRE, *and* NORA DAVID *(all 2003).*

The glass panels have been slightly frosted to show the background brickwork less obtrusively. The intensity of this background also matters: we change the colouring of letters accordingly, e.g. Nora David here.

This spiral path
to the stone circle
carved by the
Cardozo Kindersley
Workshop marks
the naming of the
MICHAEL YOUNG CENTRE
27 OCTOBER 2001

Further in, toward the rail tracks, there is a remarkable circle of 12 stones from 2001, with a huge one in the middle saying CENTRE. Each member of the circle bears a single different letter for MICHAEL YOUNG, and all were carved in situ. The first intention had been to use runic letters; what developed in the cutting instead were entirely original bold new capitals.

This work was done in Rattee & Kett's old stonemasons' yard; Lida spent some time choosing usable large boulders from those left behind. Putting each one upright in the correct place within the circle was a major undertaking – they are massive. She also found a good Portland stone for the spiral path inscription. At the time the place thronged with students, and there was a water feature for the central boulder, to make a convivial campus scene.

Morley Memorial School (Blinco Grove)

The 1989 Portland stone for DOROTHY HURST LAID THIS STONE is on an outside wall to the right of the entrance.

The school dates from 1900; 100 years on in 2000 it celebrated both the millennium and its initials with MM at the centre of a marble run: *'A good beginning'* is the school motto.

Another Portland stone with unpainted letters – weathering is to take its course.

This York stone was set into the playground; the school motto has been worked into continuous lettering for allowing marbles a clear run from the A to the centre.

Perse School (Hills Road)

*The sports centre shows a blue-grey slate naming THE ALEX
COOK CENTRE (2008). Note the elongated letter form; here
a staging post leading up to the design of a typeface called
Pulle in 2010.*

Classic lettering on this outside stone fulfills four functions: it names the building, explains about refurbishing, records the opening, and finishes with the benefactors in italics.

Strangeways Research Laboratory (Worts Causeway, Cambridge CB1 8RN)

An opening plaque for ...THESE NEWLY REFURBISHED LABORATORIES... is a Welsh slate of 1999, on an outside wall facing south-west. Another Welsh slate is indoors, naming the Raymond and Beverly Sackler Research Laboratory (2004).

RAYMOND & BEVERLY SACKLER RESEARCH LABORATORY

St Thomas's Hall (Ancaster Way, Cambridge CB1 3TT)

Lovely 1980 glass doors TO THE GLORY OF GOD... are just beyond the entrance.

For these panels, reversed lettering was drawn straight onto the glass with a felt-tip pen, and then engraved using a dentist's drill. This is a slow process, and all done by hand; fixing the panes in the church is the final step. Whilst making photographs for our archive, David was caught passing by! The extensive Workshop archive has every commission recorded in detail, with its documents, designs and photographs.

IN LOVING MEMORY OF VIOLET AMY WILLIAMS, SECOND
DAUGHTER OF GEORGE EDWARD PEARCE-SEROCOLD
1868-1943 ∅ AND OF HER HUSBAND JOHN ROBERT
STEWART WATKIN WILLIAMS 1863-1935 ∅ ALSO THEIR
SON JOSEPH SEROCOLD STEWART WILLIAMS 1899-1946
RESIDENTS OF BRITISH COLUMBIA FOR MANY YEARS
AND ALSO OF THEIR DAUGHTER
MARJORIE ALINE STEWART WILLIAMS 1901-1985 ∅

In memory of four PEARCE-SEROCOLD brothers
COL· OSWALD·CMG·VD·DL·1865 ∅ 1951
BRIG-GEN·ERIC· CMG ·1870 ∅ 1926
CHARLES SEYMOUR·1872 ∅ 1914
CDR· CLAUD·OBE·RNVR·1875 ∅ 1959
Descendants of Ralph Serocold of Hinton d·1668

Cherry Hinton

Uphill at the northern outskirts, St Andrew's
church has two Welsh slates inside under the
tower. 'In memory of four PEARCE-SEROCOLD
brothers...' (1990) recalls a family with a 300 year
Cherry Hinton history. The Serocold name is also
among those of a 1986 tablet for VIOLET AMY
WILLIAMS, her husband, son and daughter.

Two Welsh slates with
long lines of small
capitals: such pieces
are a severe test of the
lettercutter's skill.
The requirements are
balance and even
texture throughout;
good spacing and
stamina are the key.

In memory of
Isabella
MACKAY
1885-1976
Duncan
MACKAY
1834-1919
&
Jane Noble
MACKAY
1833-1917

MANU FORTI

Three names from a well known Cambridge hardware store family, together with their clan mark, had all to be got onto a single stone – a challenge demanding tight margins and a strong design. After all, 'if you cut it in stone you want it to last'.

In the churchyard there is a 1977 headstone in Welsh blue-black slate for three MACKAY family members (south-west fringe).

Clipsham stone invites lichen, and over the years the horizontal aspect has become illegible, whilst the vertical sides have preserved the name.

There is also a much overgrown ledgerstone for *BERTRAM LLEWELLYN BOSTON* (mid-northern fringe). This is a 2 metre-long Clipsham stone of 1947, inscribed on the sides.

Abbey

The Newmarket Road cemetery is huge; scattered among the many memorials are four headstones by the Workshop (the office in the south-west corner of the cemetery is a ready resource for locations – all the names are in the list at the end).

Four slates showing different solutions for different people.

LOCKE is for a child, with several letters nesting; 'The sweetest bravest boy' is from his favourite story 'The Very Hungry Caterpillar'. SMITH is in flowing italics, and contrasts with the capitals for MANNI. THURBON illustrates that lettering design is the dominant feature here, not stone shape.

A 1946 Cornish granite cross for REGINALD ANTONY LEN-
DON SMITH is on the immediate right of the metalled path
leading in a northerly direction from the office, about two thirds
of the south-north length of the cemetery. It is the first of David
Kindersley's Cambridge pieces, described in 'The start' at the
beginning of the book (on page 15).

Chesterton

St Andrew's Road had a magnificent 1½ metre-high coloured coat of arms on the building of Pye (Cambridge) Ltd. After it was carved in 1973 the firm was fulsome in its praise ('words beggar description') – but now it is lost.

This huge coat of arms was carved by several people – the team in the Workshop combining to advantage. It shows great depth in the relief. Armorial symbols are about recognition on the battlefield, loud and brash, so colouring is essential. At the top left the gilded beast holds the Y from PYE; the large blue Y in the middle is a pall, and a rare feature in secular (as opposed to ecclesiastical) heraldry.

PRECISION PROGRESS

AND

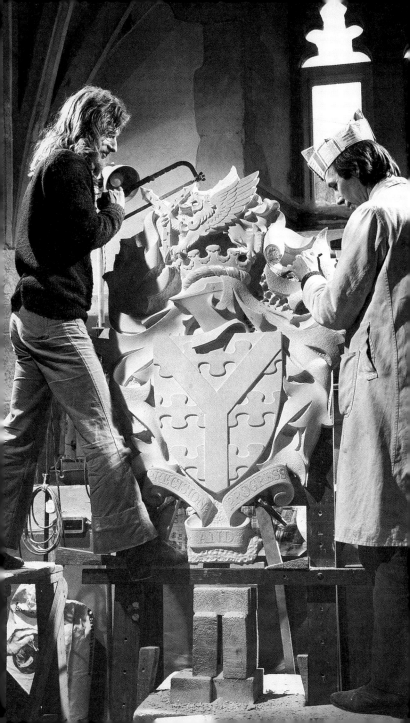

Chesterton church
On the wall to the left of the altar, a Welsh slate (1952) is for WILLIAM LEAVERS MACKENNAL,

Archdeacon of Ely. At the other end of the church, under the tower, look up at the inscription hewn into the stone: SPIRE TOWER CHANCEL RESTORED 1968.

In the churchyard there are two Welsh slate cremation tablets in the ground on turning left as you leave the church: ELIZABETH BARKLEY (1991) and BASIL ROBERTS BUCHANAN & ELENE (1988/2005).

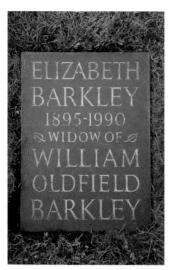

The leaves by 'widow of' in BARKLEY are derivative of Eric Gill; contrast this stone with longer names and dates for BUCHANAN which dictate design and choice of letter form.

Carving in situ always allows us an extra dimension: freedom to integrate lettering into an inspiring space.

Spire
Tower
Chancel
Restored 1968

The Workshop, March 2011

Just inside the church's main entrance, on the left, is REMEMBER BERTHA GARNER: a 1980 Portland stone with letters painted light red. The churchyard behind the altar, next to the Workshop, has a cremation plaque in the ground for DAVID ROBERT GRIFFITH HARDIE, an Elterwater green slate on a Portland stone base (2009). And near it is a Welsh slate also on a Portland plinth: the 1998 ledgerstone for DAVID GUY BARNABAS KINDERSLEY. He looks out on his Workshop.

Remember
BERTHA
GARNER
S·R·N
1884 - 1978
For many years a
devoted worshipper
at St. Luke's Church

'A boy of a hundred skills/talents' is the Latin for this much loved young man.

97

Remember
David Guy
Barnards
Kindersley
Sculptor
Lettercutter
Inventor
Born 11 June 1915
Died 2 Feb 1995
Husband of
Lida Helena
Lopes Cardozo
Lettercutter

the worker
is hidden in the
workshop

David loved flourishes!
The base round it has 'The
moving finger writes, and
having writ, moves on' from the
Rubaiyat of Omar Khayyam.

Histon Road cemetery

It can also be entered from Victoria Road, and has two headstones: *CATHARINE OLGA KORNICKI (Elterwater green slate, 1996)* – turn left after the Histon Road entrance; and *THOMAS JØRGENSEN (Portland stone, 2006)*.

Workshop picture of the still uncompleted Portland stone, as it appears fresh from the quarry before weathering

Castle (with Arbury)

St Giles/Ascension ground ,just north of Storey's Way, is a very quiet cemetery reached by foot on a metalled path from the Huntingdon Road. There are 15 Workshop stones here; 11 are illustrated, and all names are in the list at the end.

ARTHUR
PECK
1902-1974
FELLOW
OF CHRIST'S
COLLEGE
1926-1974
SOMETIME
SQUIRE OF
THE
MORRIS RING
✝
ΚΥΡΙΕ ΕΛΕΗΣΟΝ

Here, and overleaf, is a range of solutions, from the strict sans serif capitals of PECK to the flowing and joyful italics for TOLLER. Decorations are also used, as in CHEAL; flourishes are exuberant for MAULE, more restrained for RIDSDILL SMITH.

MARJORIE
Died 22 January
1991 aged 84 yrs
wife of
Arnold Duncan
McNAIR

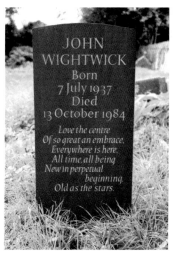

JOHN
WIGHTWICK
Born
7 July 1937
Died
13 October 1984

*Love the centre
Of so great an embrace,
Everywhere is here,
All time, all being
New in perpetual
    beginning.
Old as the stars.*

GEOFFREY
RIDSDILL
SMITH
29 JANUARY 1898
16 JULY 1992
and his wife
MARY ALICE
née MITCHELL
22 JUNE 1904
5 JANUARY 1992

Remembered in love

EVELYN
GERTRUDE
ROBERTSON
BELOVED WIFE
AND MOTHER
15 OCTOBER
15 JANUARY 1967
BLESSED ARE
THE PURE IN HEART
FOR THEY SHALL SEE

TOLLER has music floating above (Purcell's Dido) and his cat Luna on the back.

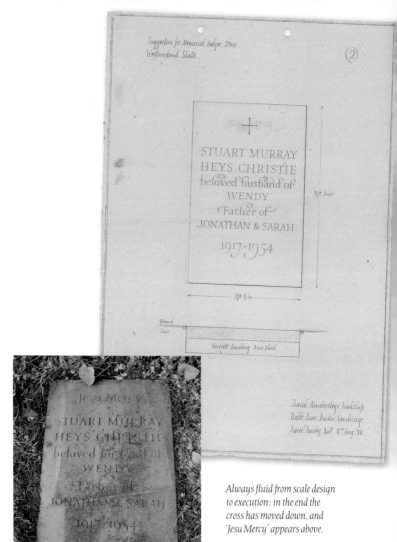

Jesu ✝ Mercy

STUART MURRAY
HEYS CHRISTIE
beloved husband of
WENDY
Father of
JONATHAN & SARAH

1917–1954

3ft 2in

2ft ½in

Ground
line

Concrete Landing 3ins thick

David Kindersley: Workshop.
Butler Court: Barton: Cambridge
David Pawsley: Bot: 8th Aug '58

*Always fluid from scale design
to execution: in the end the
cross has moved down, and
'Jesu Mercy' appears above.*

There is also a large stone against the wall of the small chapel, to the right of the entrance door: *ALPHABET MUSEUM AND SEMINAR* in red letters above an array of capitals below (Welsh slate, 1959). It was commissioned by David Diringer, of the remarkable 'The Alphabet: a key to the History of Mankind' (London, Hutchinson, 3rd rev. ed. 1968). The museum he had planned in Cambridge, later Tel Aviv, was incomplete at his death (1975).

This slate had been planned to go indoors, because the top lettering was painted black, and the design below off-white. Black would not have shown up out of doors in the wet (much of the time in Cambridge!). At some stage the paint was cleaned off, and the title above coloured red.

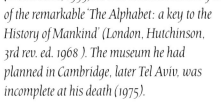

At the approach from Huntingdon Road there is a freestanding green slate in a lawn on the left for HENRY MORRIS, County Education Secretary (1989).

Green slate inscription for a famed Cambridge educationalist. Green slate of Cumbria and Westmorland has its origins in volcanic ash which fell into the still lagoons of north-west England aeons ago. Its homogeneous composition contrasts with other slates, e.g. Welsh: made up of mud and clay. (See David Kindersley & Lida Lopes Cardozo 'Letters Slate Cut', Cambridge 2004).

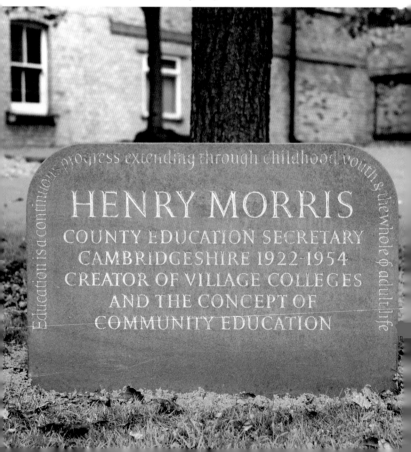

Education is a continuous progress extending through childhood youth & the whole of adult life

HENRY MORRIS
COUNTY EDUCATION SECRETARY
CAMBRIDGESHIRE 1922-1954
CREATOR OF VILLAGE COLLEGES
AND THE CONCEPT OF
COMMUNITY EDUCATION

Compare with the Cambridge University Press war memorial (page 70), also in walnut, painted and gilded. This is more expensive, using the full heraldic achievement with motto, shield, helmet, mantling, torse, crest and, in the county's case, supporters too. Mantling is a very versatile design element, and can be made into any shape.

To the memory of
John BAXTER Robert Alfred
Walter DAWKINS Frank
Holgate HANCOCK William
Dick HAWKES William
Reginald JARMAN David
Herbert SHIPP members of
the Shire Hall staff who died in the
Great War 1939-1945
We shall remember them

Inside the lobby a staircase on the right has a fine 1950 Australian walnut tablet TO THE MEMORY OF: a Second World War memorial to Shire Hall staff. Upstairs the Honours Board outside the Council Chamber had an addition by David Kindersley in 1968: the carved county coat of arms on top, in American walnut.

The county coat of arms, carved in the Workshop to be placed above the existing board; cheerful yet admirable in its restraint.

107

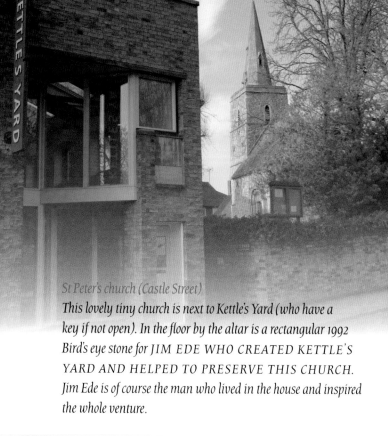

St Peter's church (Castle Street)

This lovely tiny church is next to Kettle's Yard (who have a key if not open). In the floor by the altar is a rectangular 1992 Bird's eye stone for JIM EDE WHO CREATED KETTLE'S YARD AND HELPED TO PRESERVE THIS CHURCH. Jim Ede is of course the man who lived in the house and inspired the whole venture.

St Giles church (bottom of Castle Street)

GWENYTH MARY JAMES is an Elterwater green slate in the floor to the right of the altar (1998). Fixing a slate of this design into an existing tiled floor is tricky: the old tiles have to be removed and the ground prepared. The Workshop sees these tasks through from A to Z.

The shape of the slate is determined by the surrounding tile floor pattern. The inscription is made to fit that diamond frame.

Church of the Good Shepherd (Mansel Way, Cambridge CB4 2ET)

In the middle of Arbury, and originally to be called the New Church of St Nicholas Ferrar, after the Little Gidding leader. But he was not a saint and the diocese did not like that; there is still a chapel for him though. The 1957 Ketton stone for the opening was laid by PRINCESS MARGARET, to be seen on the outside south-east wall. The beginning is short for 'Ad Majorem Dei Gloriam'.

This Ketton stone is outside in a protected setting, and lasts well anyway. Cambridge has no stone supplies of its own, apart from clunch, so everything has to be imported – the Ketton stone from Leicestershire.

HIS ROYAL HIGHNESS
THE PRINCE PHILIP
DUKE of EDINBURGH KG KT
OPENED THIS BUILDING
7 MAY 1976

Newnham

High Cross site (Madingley Road)
The British Antarctic Survey (furthest west on this site) has a fine 1976 opening stone HIS ROYAL HIGHNESS THE PRINCE PHILIP... in the floor of Science Block 1, the old reception area. It is Antarctic granite, brought to Cambridge in 1975 after being hewn in the vicinity of the former BAS station at Prospect Point in Graham Land.

Dr Raymond Adie of the British Antarctic Survey brought this specially selected slab to Cambridge in 1975 – transporting it across the ice was an unusual task for his team. The flecked material is unique as a base for Workshop inscriptions. The record of its retrieval is reproduced by courtesy of British Antarctic Survey Archives Service. Ref. no. WA/PH22 (1975) Copyright: Natural Environment Research Council.

THE SCHOOL OF
VETERINARY MEDICINE
WAS OPENED BY
HER MAJESTY
QUEEN ELIZABETH II
on the twentieth day
of October 1955
HER MAJESTY
WAS ACCOMPANIED BY
HIS ROYAL HIGHNESS
THE DUKE of EDINBURGH

The 1955 opening of the Veterinary School ...BY HER
MAJESTY QUEEN ELIZABETH II is celebrated by a large
carving, done directly into the building's Portland stone.
It is left in the main entrance hall. Inside the rear of the Small
Animals Hospital (south of this building) there is a 1994
gilded Welsh slate for the opening of the small animals wing
by ...THE QUEEN... .

Care is needed in the use of flourishes: when ill conceived they can look
like spaghetti and become irritating distractions. Real understanding
of where the weight lies in a flourish is important for good design.

This is really a picture and frame
made integral to this wall – but it is
a picture of letters.

To commemorate the visit of
HRH The Duke of Edinburgh KG · KT · Hon LLD
Chancellor of the University of Cambridge
on 23 June 2003
accompanied by Sir Alec Broers ScD · FRS · FREng
Emeritus Professor of Electrical Engineering
Vice-Chancellor 1996-2003

Interesting contrast: one glass panel is fixed by wire, as if suspended in space; the other is firmly set into its door.

Large etched glass nameplates can be found over the main entrances to the WILLIAM GATES BUILDING (2002) and the ROGER NEEDHAM BUILDING (2003). These are in or off J J Thomson Avenue, as is the Nanosciences block. The latter has a glass panel (2004) for the visit of HRH THE DUKE OF EDINBURGH, to the right in the entrance lobby; also an engraved glass door to 'The Wolfson Clean Rooms' (2004) further down a corridor to the right.

A privately owned sundial nearby. Each dial must be calibrated specially for its site. The Latin is 'The times change and we change with them'.

Moore Library (Wilberforce Road)

The 2003 glass opening plaque ...BETTY & GORDON MOORE is on a wall to the left, opposite the reception desk.

The two lines have capitals of different sizes, so the typography accentuates the generosity of the benefactors.

THE BUILDING OF THIS LIBRARY WAS MADE POSSIBLE BY
THE GENEROSITY OF BETTY & GORDON MOORE

The Lauterpacht Research Centre for International Law
(5/7 Cranmer Road)

The outside of no.7 has two 2003 Welsh slates, one naming
the Centre, the other *BAHRAIN HOUSE*. At the back of no.5
there is a terrace with curved York stone steps where *OUR
PRINCIPAL BENEFACTORS... was cut in situ (1997); with
the additions of HIS MAJESTY THE KING OF BAHRAIN
(2003) and MALAYSIA (2007).*

*These slates stand out well on their red bricks.
The v-cut frames around the edges define the
central inscriptions.*

116

...CENTURY AT HERACHT·EARL·SNYDER·JULIE·FINLEY·TRINITY·COLLEGE

OUR·PRINCIPAL·BENEFACTORS

The whole of the Workshop team were on their knees cutting this inscription. Thank goodness it doesn't rain every day in Cambridge.

Her Majesty The Queen opened this building for the Faculty of Divinity on 23 November 2000

THIS BUILDING was made possible by contributions from the University of Cambridge·Cambridge University Press·the Local Examinations Syndicate & the Isaac Newton Trust·St John's, Jesus, Selwyn & Emmanuel Colleges & the KBE & the Hinduja Foundations·the Habib Bank·the Mulberry·Homestead·Eling·Golden Bottle·RM Sturdy·Forte & Joseph Rank Benevolent Trusts & the Girdlers' and Mercers' Companies & HarperCollins·Random House·the Bible Society·Epworth Press & and many members of the University of Cambridge and further afield

Divinity Faculty (West Road)
In 2000 HER MAJESTY THE QUEEN OPENED THIS BUILDING – *a round Welsh slate to the right in the entrance lobby. Beneath it is another but rectangular slate for benefactors (2000). The curved glass of the entrance bears divinity quotations in various languages, etched in the same year.*

The benefactors on their rectangle are in sober factual mode; contrast this with the exuberant roundel above, celebrating the opening in gilded letters and flourishes.

Seven languages – the lines are given in the order of their appearance from up to down, on left then right doors.

ARABIC: And above every learned one there is one Learned
SYRIAC: The thought of truth led me and I went after it and did not go astray
LATIN: Wisdom has built herself a house
ENGLISH: Teach one another in all wisdom
HEBREW: Let the wise listen and add to their learning
GREEK: In the beginning was the Word
SANSKRIT: Everything reflects Him, while it is He alone who shines

English Faculty (West Road)

The 2005 opening by HER MAJESTY THE QUEEN
is celebrated on a diamond slate on a wall just beyond the
entrance. A glass plate for 'The Garfield Weston Foundation',
also 2005, can be found in a ground floor corridor to the north.
NEWMAN'S CORNER IN MEMORY OF HARRY
NEWMAN is a 2006 glass plaque in green on the first floor of
the library.

Letters painted off-white are set in a
gold line to contrast with the concrete
wall behind.

THE
GARFIELD
WESTON
FOUNDATION
GENEROUSLY
·FUNDED·
TH·SE·
R·O·OMS

Note that glass panels set away from the wall give at once another dimension.

NEWMANS CORNER
IN MEMORY OF
HARRY NEWMAN
1921–2001
M· LITT·
S· JOHNS COLLEGE
1946–1949
ENTREPRENEUR
POET

This elongated lettering was hand-drawn and has since been made into a typeface called Pulle (2010).

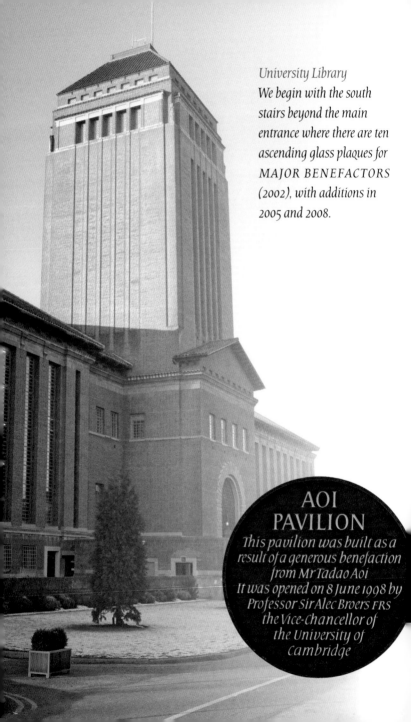

University Library
We begin with the south
stairs beyond the main
entrance where there are ten
ascending glass plaques for
MAJOR BENEFACTORS
(2002), with additions in
2005 and 2008.

AOI
PAVILION
This pavilion was built as a
result of a generous benefaction
from Mr Tadao Aoi
It was opened on 8 June 1998 by
Professor Sir Alec Broers FRS
the Vice-Chancellor of
the University of
Cambridge

Benefactors line the route up the staircase on entry, in parade order on the way to the books.

On the first floor (south) the AOI Pavilion has a 1998 glass plate naming it on a wall; down a flight of stairs is the pavilion's opening stone of the same year, a Welsh slate roundel.

At the north end of the first floor the refurbished MAP ROOM and its benefactor is on a 2008 glass plaque in green lettering.

This room is dedicated to
THE ROYAL COMMONWEALTH SOCIETY LIBRARY

From its foundation in 1868, the organisation known successively as the Colonial Society, the Royal Colonial Institute, the Royal Empire Society and currently the Royal Commonwealth Society (R.C.S.) amassed a unique collection of books, manuscripts & photographs of the British Empire, the Commonwealth and its many member countries and territories. *ø ø ø ø ø*
At the beginning of the 1990s, the R.C.S. faced a severe financial crisis and was forced to contemplate the sale & dispersal of the library collection. An appeal, launched in 1992 with The Prince of Wales as Patron and Sir Patrick Sheehy as its Chairman, saved the R.C.S. Library collections for the nation and enabled them to be moved to Cambridge University Library. Here they continue to grow and are available to researchers and the general public from around the world.

TO COMMEMORATE THE VISIT BY HIS ROYAL HIGHNESS
THE PRINCE OF WALES ON 27th MAY 2008

On the third floor (south-west corner) there is the Commonwealth Room, with a large 2006 slate THE ROYAL COMMONWEALTH SOCIETY LIBRARY... The 2008 visit of HRH THE PRINCE OF WALES is commemorated on another Welsh slate below it.

124

A stone with a huge text: we spent around 70 days in solid cutting; each letter takes about 1000 blows of the hammer. Keeping rhythm and evenness going for such a task is the lettercutter's life – continuously adapting letter forms and spacing.

HAEC CAMERA
STANLEII MORISON
NOMEN PERPETVAT
BIBLIOTHECAM TVTATVR
PER MVNIFICENTIAM
ALLENI LANE
EQVITIS AVRATI
AD MCMLXVIII

This slate celebrates a great 20th century typographer in the classic tradition, whose papers are in the University Library. He supervised the design of Times New Roman, commissioned by The Times in 1931.

We end with the Morison Room, part of the exhibition centre on the ground floor of the North Front. A 1976 rectangular Welsh slate HAEC CAMERA…. is for Stanley Morison. On the wall opposite hang a series of eight Welsh slates (2000): they reflect 2500 years of script, books, libraries and letter forms. The texts were chosen by Cambridge academics of many disciplines. At the time, thinking through this commission from the Librarian Peter Fox, we considered using differing shapes and materials for each panel. The final decision was for squares of Welsh slate throughout (46 × 46 cm). Depicting these steps of cultural development over two and a half millennia needed external coherence. The huge variety of styles covered could best be put into the internal design and letter forms for each slate; from the angular certainty of the Old Testament to Eric Gill's questing capitals, which read across and then up. This is human history: of literacy.

HEBREW: Of making many books there is no end.
Ecclesiastes 12:12, circa 3rd century BCE

GREEK: In the beginning was the word.
Gospel according to St John 1:1, circa 1st century

LATIN: The word when written endures.
Etymologiae 1:3, 7th century

LITTERA SCRIPTA MANET

CAROLINE MINUSCULE: ...only letters are immortal and ward off death, only letters in books bring the past to life. Indeed God's hand carved letters on the rock that pleased Him when He gave His law to the people, and these letters reveal everything in the world that is, has been, or may chance to come in the future. From a poem on scribes by Hrabanus Maurus, Archbishop of Mainz, mid 9th century

BLACK-LETTER: Libraries are the most precious monuments of mankind. Günther Weisenborn, Memorial, mid 20th century

ITALIC: A man will turn over half a library to make one book. Dr Johnson, (James Boswell, The Life of Samuel Johnson), late 18th century

COPPERPLATE: Read in order to live. Gustave Flaubert, Letter to Mlle Leroyer de Chantepie, mid 19th century

NOT PICTURES OF THINGS

LETTERS ARE THINGS

SANS SERIF: Letters are
things not pictures of things.
Eric Gill, Typography, mid
20th century

Churchyards & burial grounds

Cherry Hinton

BERTRAM LLEWELLYN BOSTON	1947	Clipsham stone
ISABELLA MACKAY & DUNCAN MACKAY & JANE NOBLE MACKAY	1977	Welsh blue-black slate

Chesterton

ELIZABETH BARKLEY	1991	Welsh slate
BASIL ROBERTS BUCHANAN husband of ELENE	1988/2005	Welsh slate

Histon Road

THOMAS JØRGENSEN	2006	Portland stone
CATHARINE OLGA KORNICKI	1996	Elterwater green slate

Newmarket Road

CONSTANCE BABINGTON SMITH	2002	Welsh slate
LOCKE GERALD NOLAN BLANCHARD	2008	Elterwater green slate
REGINALD ANTONY LENDON SMITH	1946	Cornish granite
BATTISTA DOMENICO MANNI and his loving wife FLORENCE ELIZABETH	1993	Welsh slate
WILLIAM THOMAS THURBON husband of ALICE ZILLAH	1994	Welsh slate

St. Botolph's Church

ARTHUR LLEWELLYN ARMITAGE and his wife JOAN KENYON	1985/2006	Welsh blue-black slate

St. Edward's Church

SIR GEOFFREY INGRAM TAYLOR and his wife STEPHANIE	1993	Green slate

St. Giles Ascension

PAULINE CHEAL	1991	Welsh slate
STUART MURRAY HEYS CHRISTIE	1959	Westmorland green slate
FLORENCE GILL	1958	Nabresina marble
DIANE HALL	2001	Mansfield White
MILDRED HUDSON	1963	Nabresina marble
PHYLLIS MADELEINE HYLIE MACGREGOR & JAMES MACGREGOR	1954	Portland stone: addition & recutting of existing letters
MARJORIE wife of ARNOLD DUNCAN MCNAIR	1972/77	Ketton stone
JEREMY FRANK MAULE	1999	Welsh slate
ARTHUR PECK	1977	Welsh blue-black slate
SIR LEON RADZINOWICZ & his darling wife ISOLDE	2000/2011	Welsh slate
GEOFFREY RIDSDILL SMITH and his wife MARY ALICE	1993	Elterwater green slate
EVELYN GERTRUDE ROBERTSON	1962	Portland stone

NICHOLAS MANNING TOLLER	2010	Elterwater green slate
JOHN WIGHTWICK	1985	Welsh slate
JOHN WISDOM	1994	Green slate

St. Luke's Church, Victoria Road

| DAVID ROBERT GRIFFITH HARDIE | 2009 | Elterwater green slate, Portland stone base |
| DAVID GUY BARNABAS KINDERSLEY | 1998 | Welsh slate on Portland stone plinth |

Trumpington churchyard (first yard, south-west corner)

Tablets

FIONA THE LADY BAKER & LORD BAKER	1980/86	Green slate
SARA BAILEY	1983	Welsh Slate
ELIZABETH RUTH BARKER	1972	Welsh slate
FREDERICK JAMES BYWATERS	1977	Welsh slate
ROBERT GARDNER and his wife MARGARET	1973	Welsh slate
ARTHUR HERBERT GRAY	1972	Welsh slate
DOROTHY ELSIE GRAY	1984	Welsh slate
HENRY CHRISTIAN NEWBERY	1957	Welsh slate
HERBERT SWAN PERKINS and his wife JANE	1977	Welsh slate

Headstone

| REGINALD GEORGE SMITH | 1973 | Portland stone |

Sir GEORGE DARWIN, MAUD DU PUY & GWENDOLINE MARY RAVERAT	1958	Welsh slate on Portland plinth
T. PERCY, PATIENCE F.S. & WILLIAM W. PEMBERTON ANNIE MASON VIOLA P.C. PEMBERTON	1962/72	Portland stone

The Workshop at work: *drawing out free-hand from scale design onto the stone, then chiselling, lastly painting or gilding – a whole sequence of tasks goes into the making of each piece. And never a computer in sight...*

THIS HOUSE WAS BUILT FOR
ROBERT & ELIZABETH HIRSCH
IN OCTOBER MCMLXXV BY
VICTOR & DEREK MEEKS
MASTER BUILDERS OF LINTON
IN CAMBRIDGESHIRE